ALIEN INVADERS

SPECIES THAT THREATEN OUR WORLD

Jane Drake & Ann Love
ILLUSTRATED BY **Mark Thurman**

TUNDRA BOOKS

This book is dedicated to the memory of our cousin Doug Stewart, who made everyone smile. – J.D. and A.L.

To Marianne, who has respect for all creatures no matter how small. – M.T.

We would like to thank Henry, Ian, and Will Barnett; Kim Bilous; Barbara Cochrane; Jane Crist; Brian, Jim, Madeline, and Stephanie Drake; Tom Drake; Ron Dueck; Allan Foster; Newt Hardy; Adrian, David, Jennifer, and Melanie Love; Geoff Love and Mimi McEvenue; Tom and Asun McGrath; Jim Miller; Marie Muir; Donna O'Connor; Evan, Luke, and Olivia Racine; Wendy Reifel; John Riley; Dave Salmoni; Mark, Mason, and Sadie Salmoni; Lisa Scott; Mary Thompson; Val Wyatt; and Pamela Zevit.

Special thanks for the detailed and expert advice offered by Dawn Bazely, Kevin Kavanagh, and Andrew Tanentzap.

Thanks to our editor, Sue Tate, who has a sharp but twinkling eye. We feel fortunate to work with Kathy Lowinger and all the good people at Tundra Books.

Text copyright © 2008 by Jane Drake and Ann Love
Illustrations copyright © 2008 by Mark Thurman

Published in Canada by Tundra Books,
75 Sherbourne Street, Toronto, Ontario M5A 2P9

Published in the United States by Tundra Books of
Northern New York,
P.O. Box 1030, Plattsburgh, New York 12901

Library of Congress Control Number: 2007927432

Library and Archives Canada Cataloguing in Publication

Drake, Jane
    Alien invaders : species that threaten our world
/ Jane Drake, Ann Love ; illustrations by Mark
Thurman.

For ages 9-12.
Includes index.
ISBN 978-0-88776-798-2

1. Introduced organisms – Juvenile literature.
2. Biological invasions – Juvenile literature.   I. Love,
Ann   II. Thurman, Mark, 1948-   III. Title.

QL83.D73 2008   j578.6'2   C2007-
902736-9

We acknowledge the financial support of the
Government of Canada through the Book
Publishing Industry Development Program (BPIDP)
and that of the Government of Ontario through the
Ontario Media Development Corporation's Ontario
Book Initiative. We further acknowledge the sup-
port of the Canada Council for the Arts and the
Ontario Arts Council for our publishing program.

 ONTARIO ARTS COUNCIL
CONSEIL DES ARTS DE L'ONTARIO

Medium: Gouache on board

Design: Jennifer Lum

Printed and bound in China

1 2 3 4 5 6   13 12 11 10 09 08

KGW

CONTENTS

WHO ARE YOU?
WHERE DID YOU COME FROM?

Millions cross oceans, clinging to ships' hulls or as stowaways in cargo holds. Thousands hitchhike on truck trailers or in packing crates. Untold numbers curl up in airplane landing gear at night, or sneak into the folds of luggage. Some even swagger across borders in broad daylight, their passage provided by unknowing, careless humans.

Once they arrive, their numbers grow, slowly at first – and silently. Then the killing begins. They strangle, suffocate, drown, sting, trample, starve, suck out the lifeblood, and even eat their victims. Only then do we notice our homeland has been invaded and we could be overwhelmed by alien invaders.

INVITED OR NOT

In 1890, Eugene Scheiffelin lovingly released sixty European starlings into New York's Central Park. He hoped to beautify the city with every bird mentioned in Shakespeare's plays – including starlings. Aggressive, comfortable near people, and with few natural predators, his starlings thrived. Ready to eat just about any bug, fruit, or seed, and happy to live on farms, in cities, even in garbage dumps, their descendants now number nearly 200 million birds across North America.

Every autumn, starlings congregate in huge flocks and swarm farmlands, devouring grain, corn, and ripe fruits.

In spring, they drive shyer birds – flickers, bluebirds, swallows – out of nesting holes, eat the eggs, and lay their own. In cities, starlings spread disease by fouling cars, balconies, handrails, and playground equipment with their droppings. If a neighborhood is well lit, roosting starlings keep everyone awake at night with their squawks. Starlings are a threat near airports, causing accidents when planes suck whole flocks into their jet engines. Today, North Americans call starlings dirty, noisy, disease-spreading pests.

Starlings are alien invaders in North America – *alien* because they come from another region, and *invaders* because they are taking over. Alien invasions begin when humans introduce plants, animals, bacteria, or viruses, deliberately or accidentally, to a new habitat. Not all introduced species survive. Some become manageable pests, like dandelions. Only a few explode in numbers, damage property, destroy habitat, and threaten extinctions. Starlings are not just introduced birds or exotics – they are too numerous and too harmful to property and wildlife. Scientists call starlings an invasive species . . . or an alien invader.

INVADER – *European Starling (alias Common Starling)*

SIZE – *21 cm (8.3 in.) long*

HOMELANDS – *Eurasia, North Africa*

INVADING – *temperate regions worldwide*

LINE OF ATTACK – *European settlers freed starlings from birdcages to fill their new gardens with birdsong from home.*

ECOGUARDIAN: THE ROLE OF A COMMUNITY ELDER

The first Europeans to explore the Oak Ridges Moraine tramped through dense, and sometimes marshy, forest. They didn't know that flowing in the ground beneath them were sixty-five river systems feeding Lake Simcoe and Lake Ontario. But they ate the salmon, wild strawberries, and mushrooms that flourished in this watershed. And they marveled at the abundant wildlife, including owls, foxes, passenger pigeons, porcupines, hares, and bears.

Wherever people put down roots, a few individuals become the keepers of their natural communities. These ecoguardians recognize what belongs, what's missing, and what's invading. And they sound the alarm when change threatens the environment.

INVADER – *Human (alias Person)*

SIZE – *average North American is 168 cm (5.5 ft.) tall, weighing 75 kg (165 lb.)*

HOMELANDS – *Africa, Asia*

INVADING – *everywhere*

LINE OF ATTACK – *on foot, by donkey, boat, train, or plane, humans have spread to all corners of the earth. As they travel, some leave behind other invasive species or take away the last remnants of native species.*

In 1958, a young father drove north from Toronto to this unspoiled moraine. At the top of a mature beech tree, he spied a red-shouldered hawk. Among the cattails beside a woodland pond, his kids found frogs, salamanders, and marsh marigolds. In the meadow, a fox den hid among the native grasses. Nearby, a loggerhead shrike, also known as a butcher-bird, skewered its prey on the sharp barb of a hawthorn bush. The prize of the day was watching a pair of eastern bluebirds bring nesting material into a hole in the crook of an apple tree. Within a week, the father bought the property.

Over the next fifty years, he became an ecoguardian and identified two hundred different bird species in his neighborhood. Last summer one hundred nested nearby, but he no longer sees shrikes, whippoorwills, or bobolinks. Until ten years ago, a parade of swallows patrolled the valley, catching countless insects. They're gone now, along with the bats. But the endangered red-shouldered hawk returns each spring.

City sprawl and global warming now threaten the Oak Ridges Moraine. Wetlands are shrinking. Pesticides on lawns mean no bugs for carnivorous birds and other creatures. Well-trimmed lawns eliminate habitat for snakes, toads, and rabbits. And gardens full of imported plants replace native vegetation eaten by local wildlife.

Now a great-grandfather and community elder, this ecoguardian connects some lost species with well-known invasions. A local heronry, where herons hang out and nest, disappeared when Dutch elm disease killed all the elms. Starlings and house sparrows chased off the bluebirds, and purple loosestrife choked out wildflowers, such as marsh marigolds. After an outbreak of gypsy moths destroyed many trees in his and the surrounding forests, trilliums and other delicate plants died in the sun. Recently, wind parachuted dog-strangling vine into the area. This nasty invasive plant twists up trees, binding and choking them. Whenever the ecoguardian finds it, he digs it out by the roots and burns the plants in his fireplace.

INVADERS CHANGE THE WORLD: CLASSIC STORIES

YES, WE'VE GOT RATS!

When archaeologists found early rattraps, they calculated that people have battled rats since 2400 B.C. In the days of sailing ships – from the early 1500s to the late 1800s – rats wreaked havoc wherever they hit land, but did the most damage on islands. Hunting by night, rats wiped out flightless birds (like the dodo) and ground-nesting birds, eating both eggs and chicks. Rats share the blame with other introduced species for the extinction of the dodo and many others.

Brown rats are smart and adaptable. They reside in a number of habitats, including woodlands, open fields, garbage dumps, sewers, and basements. They'll eat almost anything, even vast quantities of cereal. Rats gobble grain in the field, in storage containers, and on board ships. Wary of changes in their environment, older rats let younger ones eat a new food to check for poison. Underground burrowers, they can gnaw through rocklike wood. And despite living an average of just one year, each female rat produces about fifty young. Scientists think there's one rat for every person on Earth. If rats were contestants on a survivor show, they'd eliminate every other species except people!

On Canada's Queen Charlotte Islands, rats took less than fifty years to finish off two kinds of seabirds and almost wipe out the tufted puffins. In 2001, when rats threatened the few remain-

ing Atlantic puffins from Puffin Island, Wales, the British military (RAF) flew in poisoned wheat, killing all the rats. It will take years for the puffins to recover – pairs raise one chick a year – if the island remains rat free.

INVADER – *Brown Rat (alias Norway Rat)*

SIZE – *about 40 cm (15.7 in.) long, including tail, and weighs 320 g (11.3 oz.)*

HOMELAND – *northern China*

INVADING – *worldwide, except Antarctica, most of the Arctic, and Alberta, Canada*

LINE OF ATTACK – *stowaways on boats since ancient times, rat "spills" occur where rats disembark down anchor chains, or along docking lines, or even by swimming ashore.*

TOAD OVERDOSE

Have you ever heard of a cure that is worse than the sickness? In 1935, plantation-owners in Australia introduced one hundred cane toads to control invasive beetles that were infesting their sugarcane. The toads didn't kill all the beetles and became giant pests themselves.

Cane toads can grow almost as big as dinner plates. The adult toads have lumpy, poisonous glands all over their skin and bulging shoulder glands that ooze venom. If dogs, cats, and small wild animals bite cane toads, they die of heart failure. Even deadly snakes – like the carpet python, black-headed python, and death adder – die trying to eat them. Cane toad eggs and tadpoles are poisonous too. A female can lay thirty thousand lethal eggs at a time, far more than most amphibians. Adult cane toads will live almost anywhere – in junk heaps, drainpipes, piles of cement blocks – as long as their home is near water, so they can wet their large bellies and lay their eggs.

Invading cane toads catch few fatal diseases. Huge, numerous, and toxic, they eat anything they can bite. They poison their predators and take over the food, water, and shelter needed by native wildlife. In parts of Australia and Guam, small animals – including frogs, lizards, and mammals – are declining in number because they can't compete with cane toad eggs, tadpoles, or adults.

INVADER – *Cane Toad (alias Marine Toad)*

SIZE – *10 to 15 cm (3.9 to 5.9 in.) long*

HOMELANDS – *South and Central America*

INVADING – *Hawaii, South Pacific islands, Australia, Caribbean islands*

LINE OF ATTACK – *in the early 1900s, cane toads were released into many tropical countries as a biological control for crop pests. They spread by hopping – expanding their range over fifty kilometers per year.*

STARVED! THE GREAT HUNGER HITS IRELAND

Some Irish people think Sir Walter Raleigh, an English explorer and poet, brought potatoes to Ireland from America in 1605. Others say the spuds washed ashore from a ship-wrecked Spanish galleon. However they arrived, potatoes soon flourished under Ireland's unique growing conditions and quickly became the main staple in the diet of the poor. A small plot of land could yield enough nutritious spuds for a large family. Most other vegetables, meats, and grains were shipped to England as payment for renting the land.

In September 1845, news spread like wildfire: An airborne powdery fungus called *Phytophthora infestans* was attacking the potato crop. The leaves of infested plants turned dark, shriveled, and rotted. When dug up, the spuds looked fine, but almost immediately some disintegrated into a stinky pulp. Others rotted in storage, infecting the surrounding healthy potatoes. Half the crop was lost, and many people starved that winter. In 1846, when there were few healthy potatoes to plant, again half the crop was lost. The fungus subsided in 1847 and there was a good harvest, but it returned in 1848.

In less than five years, about a million Irish people died from starvation, diarrhea, and "famine fever." Over another million fled to Canada and the United States on "coffin ships," many dying en route under horrible conditions. Those who survived the voyage found that the potato blight was there ahead of them.

INVADER – *Potato Blight (alias Late Blight)*

SIZE – *microscopic*

HOMELAND – *Andes Mountains of Peru, in South America*

INVADING – *North America, Europe, Russia*

LINE OF ATTACK – *the Spanish imported potatoes from Peru in the 1570s. Phytophthora infestans, a potato-destroying fungus, probably traveling in loads of potatoes, attacked North American crops in the early 1840s and spread through Irish potato fields in 1845.*

TEN OF THE MOST UNWANTED

WALKING CATFISH

Walking catfish are slick escape artists. They have stiff spines in their pectoral (chest) fins, which they use to grip onto land while they flex their bodies side to side and wriggle away like snakes. Most fish die out of water because they can't breathe, but walking catfish have special lunglike organs to breathe fresh air for short sprints.

Fish farmers and ornamental pool suppliers who breed imported walking catfish often keep them in ponds near wild wetlands. Some captive catfish literally walk to freedom, where they find food and places to build their underwater nests. The males increase the survival rates by guarding both eggs and free-swimming young from predators. In parts of south Florida, walking catfish are so plentiful, they number over fourteen thousand per hectare of wetland – that's a fish every eight square feet, about the area of your closet.

Walking catfish are nighttime bottom-feeders and eat anything they can stir up, including fish eggs, small fish, tadpoles, insects, and plants. Florida scientists worry that walking catfish are eating so many tadpoles, they threaten some species of frogs. Walking catfish not only devour most food available for wild fish, but they also eat minnows. Sometimes they even return at night from the wild to poach small fish in the same farm ponds or ornamental pools from which their forebears escaped.

INVADER – *Walking Catfish (alias Clarias Catfish)*

SIZE – *30 to 60 cm (1 to 2 ft.) long*

HOME WATERS – *lakes and rivers in eastern India, Sri Lanka, Bangladesh, Myanmar, Indonesia, Singapore*

INVADING – *Thailand, China, Taiwan, Guam, Philippines, Papua New Guinea, United States*

LINE OF ATTACK – *long ago, east Asian farmers imported walking catfish from neighboring countries to grow in fishponds. In the 1960s, American fish farmers and ornamental pond and aquarium dealers started importing walking catfish too. In both cases, the catfish broke loose and bolted into nearby ponds and streams.*

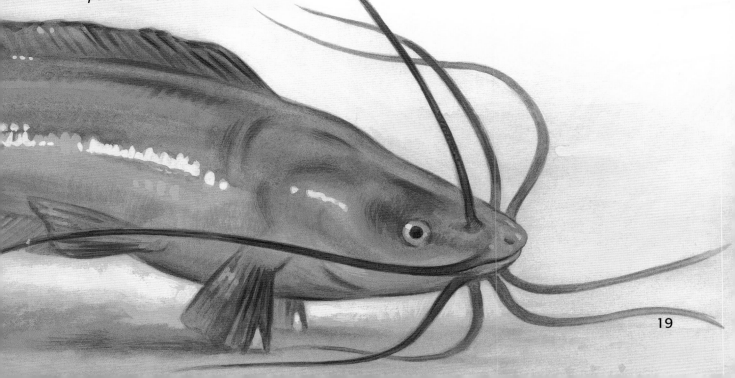

WILD CATS

"That will be $84.76," says the pet-store clerk, as he stuffs a collar with a bell, kitty litter, a pooper-scooper, kibble, catnip, and a feather toy into the bag. The new owner explains that his kitten was abandoned. "She was just skin and bones when we found her. And so scared, but our veterinarian says she'll be fine."

Not all wild cats are so lucky.

In the United States, most of the 60 million domesticated cats will live between fifteen and eighteen years. But the estimated 40-70 million wild cats will survive less than three. As the most carnivorous of all mammals, wild cats kill billions of creatures around the world every year. And because they eat fresh meat and drink blood, they require little water. Night or day, prowling cats snatch eggs or young from surprised ground-nesting and feeding birds, such as towhees, cardinals, and white-crowned sparrows. They eat lizards, mice, praying mantises, baby squirrels, and butterflies. In fact, wild cats gulp down almost anything that moves, depleting common and rare species alike.

When sailors left cats behind on small islands, these new predators hunted for survival and caused the extinction of many birds and mammals. In Tasmania, off the coast of Australia, and on islands off South Africa, feral cats have been so successful that local conservationists are poisoning or sterilizing them to protect other species. Drastic "people" solutions for a "people-caused" problem.

INVADER – *Wild Cat (alias Feral Cat)*

SIZE – *male averages 4.5 kg (9.9 lb.), female 3 kg (6.6 lb.)*

HOMELAND – *eastern Mediterranean, including Cyprus and Egypt*

INVADING – *most inhabited places on Earth*

LINE OF ATTACK – *domesticated about three thousand years ago, cats were taken on board ships to control rat populations. Lost or let loose everywhere, they landed on their feet. Amazing hunting skills made them switch from being pets to wild species.*

BROWN TREE SNAKES

"We're squared away and good to go," drawls the pilot. "Next stop, Guam!" Down the runway, the cargo plane groans, lifts off, and heads for the clouds. The copilot stows the landing gear, unaware of the hitchhiking snake he's now got on board.

Guam has the largest concentration of brown tree snakes in the world. Some parts are so densely populated, they have thirty-eight snakes in an area the size of a soccer field. Over the years, these nighttime predators have swallowed native birds, lizards, and rodents. The first to go were the flightless birds, including Guam's national bird, the near-extinct koko. When local prey became scarce, the snakes ate other introduced species, such as farm animals and caged birds. Tree snakes climb with ease and devour tree-dwelling birds, their young, and their eggs as well as small mammals, such as bats and lizards.

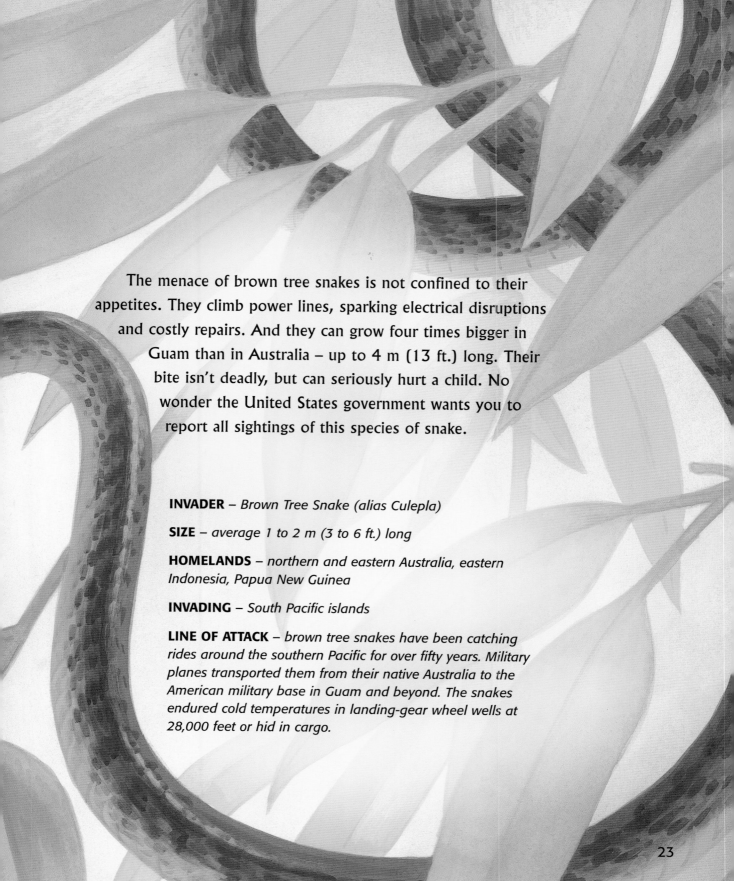

The menace of brown tree snakes is not confined to their appetites. They climb power lines, sparking electrical disruptions and costly repairs. And they can grow four times bigger in Guam than in Australia – up to 4 m (13 ft.) long. Their bite isn't deadly, but can seriously hurt a child. No wonder the United States government wants you to report all sightings of this species of snake.

INVADER – *Brown Tree Snake (alias Culepla)*

SIZE – *average 1 to 2 m (3 to 6 ft.) long*

HOMELANDS – *northern and eastern Australia, eastern Indonesia, Papua New Guinea*

INVADING – *South Pacific islands*

LINE OF ATTACK – *brown tree snakes have been catching rides around the southern Pacific for over fifty years. Military planes transported them from their native Australia to the American military base in Guam and beyond. The snakes endured cold temperatures in landing-gear wheel wells at 28,000 feet or hid in cargo.*

YELLOW CRAZY ANTS AND GIANT AFRICAN SNAILS

Crazy ants subdue prey by spraying acid in their eyes. These invasive insects nearly wiped out the red land crab, unique to Christmas Island. The ants ate the blinded crabs and then built supercolonies in the crabs' vacant burrows. Other native species, such as snails, clams, and spiders, were also overwhelmed by these acid-spraying ants. With fewer creatures eating fruits and seeds, shrub, tree, and weed populations exploded. Many birds, reptiles, and small mammals struggled as the food web changed. Finally, in 2002, the Australian government dropped toxic bait from helicopters, killing off most of the crazy ants. But the remaining few are rebuilding their colonies.

INVADER – *Yellow Crazy Ant (alias Long-Legged Ant)*

SIZE – *5 mm (.2 in.) long*

HOMELAND – *Africa or Asia, origin not certain*

INVADING – *northern Australia and nearby islands, southern United States, islands in the Caribbean Sea and Indian Ocean*

LINE OF ATTACK – *passing ships likely brought yellow crazy ants to the remote Australian territory of Christmas Island in the East Indian Ocean over seventy years ago. Gradually the ants took over nearly one quarter of the island's rain forest.*

In tropical conditions and without natural enemies, each invading giant African snail lays up to twelve hundred eggs a year. Its huge numbers and giant size add up to a big problem: Not only do giant African snails demolish at least five hundred kinds of plants, but they also eat the stucco and paint on buildings. And wherever these snails are established, local tree snails are threatened or become extinct.

People make matters worse by smuggling snails into new territory for pets or as exotic food. African giant snails are dangerous road hazards, carry parasites, and spread disease.

INVADER – *Giant African Snail (alias Giant African Land Snail)*

SIZE – *rounded shell measures 7 to 8 cm (2.7 to 3.1 in.) tall and twice as wide*

HOMELAND – *East Africa*

INVADING – *Asia, India, southern United States, South America, islands in the Pacific and Indian oceans and the Caribbean Sea*

LINE OF ATTACK – *giant African snails hitch rides in produce, luggage, and attached to vehicles.*

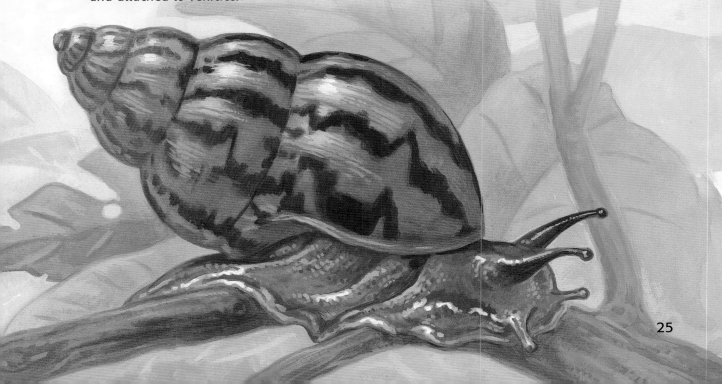

RED-EARED SLIDERS AND HYDRILLA

Cute when small, red-eared sliders grow a shell bigger than most family aquariums. When released into nature, these turtles gobble up water plants, dragonfly larvae, crayfish, frogs, toads, salamanders, and small fish. But the worst impact comes from their passion for basking in the sun. They bully water-birds off egg-filled nests and then spread out their reptile legs, neck, and tail to absorb the warm rays. Sliders weigh more than adult waterbirds, so they press the bird eggs underwater and drown them. In France and California, red-eared sliders threaten endangered native turtles by outcompeting them for food and by staking out the best basking spots.

INVADER – *Red-Eared Slider (alias Slider Turtle)*

SIZE – *20 cm (7.9 in.), nose to tail*

HOME WATERS – *Mississippi River in the United States*

INVADING – *Southeast Asia, islands in the Caribbean Sea, western United States, France, Israel, Bahrain*

LINE OF ATTACK – *since the 1970s, turtle farmers have raised red-eared sliders for international pet sales. Softhearted owners release their sliders into the wild when they outgrow their tanks.*

Invisible at first from shore, hydrilla grows from the bottom of a wetland up, at the rate of 2.5 cm (1 in.) a day. When it breaks the surface, the lake or river is filled with weed. Mats of hydrilla

smother other water plants and the animals depending on them. Hydrilla interferes with swimmers, tangles boat motors, and chokes streams, creating stagnant water where mosquitoes can breed. As it costs thousands of dollars to clean a small lake of weed, governments are battling to keep hydrilla out of the Great Lakes.

INVADER – *Hydrilla (alias Water Thyme)*

SIZE – *9 m (29.5 ft.) long*

HOME WATERS – *lakes and rivers in south India, Korea, north Australia*

INVADING – *every continent but Antarctica*

LINE OF ATTACK – *now banned for import in most countries, hydrilla was once sold worldwide as an aquarium plant. It escaped into wetlands during aquarium cleanouts and was spread by water currents, on boat and fishing gear, and in bird poop. Hydrilla still slips across borders in shipments of water lilies.*

EUROPEAN GREEN CRABS

Mottled red and orange, the European green crab is well camouflaged by rocks and sea grasses. It gobbles mussels, snails, oysters, scallops, clams, marine worms, even smaller crabs. And with a brain less than the size of a pinhead, it can learn, by experience, better ways to open shells and get at the meat. A green crab tolerates a range of water temperatures and concentrations of saltiness, but prefers shallow water to avoid the tentacles of its archenemy, the octopus.

One female lays two hundred thousand eggs, which can survive for two months if stranded out of water. And larval crabs can live eighty days while currents spread them along a coastline. Although adult green crabs are ferocious predators, they are too small for people to bother shelling.

In North America, green crabs first wiped out the soft-shell clam industry and many scallop beds in New England and Nova Scotia. Then, in 1989, they appeared on the West Coast, in San Francisco Bay, and since have invaded north to British Columbia, threatening shellfish all up the coast.

Scientists can import a parasite barnacle from the green crab's home waters as a control. This barnacle pierces the crab's shell and takes root in its guts. From there, it takes over the reproductive system of the crab to produce more barnacles.

Because the barnacles may also attack native crabs, scientists have to consider which is worse – the European green crab invasion or a possible barnacle invasion sequel.

INVADER – *European Green Crab (alias Joe Rocker)*

SIZE – *60 mm (2.4 in.) long*

HOME WATERS – *North and Baltic seas*

INVADING – *coastlines of North America, South Africa, Japan, Australia*

LINE OF ATTACK – *in the early 1800s, European green crabs spread from port to port, hidden inside crevices on ships' hulls and under rocks used to balance cargo. Green crabs are now staging secondary invasions in ballast water – used to steady ships in ocean swells – and in seaweed – used for packing live lobsters, oysters, and bait.*

PURPLE LOOSESTRIFE

A beautiful but deadly invader of marshes and moist meadows, purple loosestrife kills by suffocation. The roots grow so fast, and in such thick webs, they choke out native grasses and plants, including common cattails and rushes. And if a loosestrife root breaks, it doesn't die but resprouts. One plant can produce two million seeds a year, sowing impenetrable stands of purple loosestrife that change the nutrient and water flow of the wetland. Native waterbirds and animals – such as ducks, wrens, terns, turtles, muskrat, and mink – can no longer find food or sheltered places to rear their young. When purple loosestrife invades pastures, even big-toothed cows find the brushy stems hard to chew.

Scientists searched Eurasia for natural predators and found two beetles that prefer nibbling purple loosestrife leaves. Wherever these beetles are released in North America, they weaken many purple loosestrife plants so they don't flower, the roots shrivel, and, in three to four years, the clumps die. A few seem to survive, even with the beetles on them – but that may be a good thing. It means that small pockets of beetles will be on the site to stop future purple loosestrife invasions. The down side? This biological control is expensive.

INVADER – *Purple Loosestrife (alias Spiked Loosestrife)*

SIZE – *up to 3 m (9.8 ft.) tall*

HOMELAND – *Eurasia*

INVADING – *Canada, United States, Australia, Ethiopia*

LINE OF ATTACK – *in the early 1800s, purple loosestrife seeds left European pastures on sailing ships, often stuck to the wool of live sheep. Settlers planted purple loosestrife to use as medicine for diarrhea, ulcers, and wounds. Once introduced, the seeds spread by water, wind, wildlife, and humans, sprouting in recently disturbed, moist soils.*

ASIAN LONG-HORNED BEETLES

In 2003, ten-year-old Keisha surfed the Internet and identified a strange, large beetle her father had found on a car at work. The entire beetle, including its long antennae, covered the palm of her little sister's hand. It was an Asian long-horned beetle.

These beetles can kill a healthy tree in just three years. Their larvae gorge on vital cells inside the trunk, riddle the wood with tunnels, disrupt sap flow, and strangle the tree from the inside. They attack many trees, such as poplar, elm, ash, birch, and chestnut, but their favorite is maple. In fact, Chinese farmers control the beetles in their orchards by leaving out maple logs as bait! Because Asian long-horned beetles have no predators outside Asia and are hidden from view most of their lives, they spread quickly and secretly. So far, invasions have been restricted to neighborhoods where shipping containers in which they travel are delivered. If these beetles ever escaped into a forest, millions of trees would die. North America's deciduous forests are worth over 50 billion dollars in lumber and maple syrup – that doesn't include every forest's value in holding soil and groundwater, cleaning air, moderating temperature, supporting wildlife, and being beautiful.

The only sure way to control an infestation of Asian long-horned beetles is chopping down and burning all the host trees. So far, workers have destroyed thousands of trees in New York and Chicago to kill these beetles. Keisha's family is credited with alerting authorities in time to halt a Toronto invasion.

INVADER – *Asian Long-Horned Beetle (alias Starry Sky Beetle)*

SIZE – *3 cm (1.2 in.) long*

HOMELANDS – *China, Korea, Japan*

INVADING – *Canada, United States, Austria, England*

LINE OF ATTACK – *stowaways on freighters, Asian long-horned beetles cross oceans in untreated wooden shipping crates, pallets, and packaging. On land, adults fly self-propelled or hitchhike on vehicles.*

COMMUNITIES UNDER SIEGE

LAKE VICTORIA: INVASION ON TWO FRONTS

Lake Victoria is the largest tropical lake in the world and, until recently, home to more than 500 species of small colorful cichlids (pronounced *sick-lids*) as well as larger fish called tilapia. By 1990, 200 species of cichlid had suddenly become extinct and 150 endangered – mostly gobbled up by the Nile perch.

At first, the huge perch provided jobs and food for lakeside people. Entire forests were cut to smoke the catch. Then soil from the treeless shores spilled into the lake, making the water rich enough to grow water hyacinth.

Water hyacinth plants can double in size every twelve days. By 1996, most of the east coast of Lake Victoria was covered with the weed. Sunlight had trouble penetrating the surface, slowing photosynthesis, which adds oxygen to the water. Huge numbers of native plants and fish died and their remains, as they decomposed, used up more oxygen in the lake.

Today, small fishing boats have trouble moving through the mats of water hyacinth. Rafts of the floating weed support poisonous snakes and disease-carrying snails and mosquitoes. Meanwhile, the Nile perch, which is too expensive for most Africans, is sold in Europe. And with few small fish to eat, the perch cannibalize their own young. What happens when there are only monster perch left? The future is uncertain, not just for Lake Victoria but for the lakeside people too.

INVADER – *Nile Perch (alias African Snook)*

SIZE – *up to 2 m (6.6 ft.) long*

HOME WATERS – *lakes and rivers in North, West, and south central Africa*

LINE OF ATTACK – *in 1954, a fisheries officer threw a pailful of Nile perch minnows into Lake Victoria, East Africa, to replace overfished native species.*

INVADER – *Water Hyacinth (alias Waterweed)*

SIZE – *up to 1 m (3.3 ft.) long*

HOME WATERS – *Amazon River in South America*

LINE OF ATTACK – *water hyacinth was introduced into Africa in the nineteenth century as an ornamental floating water plant. Escaped plants drifted into Lake Victoria by river in 1990.*

HAWAII: PARADISE LOST

Invading feral pigs, mosquitoes, and a parasite show no respect for glorious Hawaii. Feral pigs scarf down anything – snails, grain, nesting seabirds and their eggs. They eat fruiting or flowering plants and spread seeds in their poop – including those of the invasive strawberry guava. The pigs excavate entire trees, but eat only the roots. When rain forms puddles in the holes left behind, pigs wallow in the cool mud and mosquitoes lay their eggs.

INVADER – *Feral Pig (alias Razorback)*

SIZE – *adult male as big as 90 kg (198.4 lb.)*

HOMELANDS – *Eurasia, North Africa*

LINE OF ATTACK – *the first pigs trotted off Polynesian ships onto the Hawaiian Islands in about 400 A.D. In 1778, Captain James Cook released a pair of European pigs. Now, large hybrid wild pigs are the most serious invasive species on the Hawaiian Islands.*

Female mosquitoes lay 150 to 200 eggs in "rafts" floating on the water. In about a week, fully formed mosquitoes pop to the surface. Females immediately search for blood, an essential ingredient for reproduction. For most humans, mosquito stings are only a nuisance; but for many birds, they are deadly.

INVADER – *Southern House Mosquito (alias Mosquito)*

SIZE – *less than 7.6 mm (.3 in.) long*

HOMELANDS – *unknown, but now lives everywhere, except Antarctica*

LINE OF ATTACK – *Hawaii was a mosquito-free zone until 1826, when sailors, on board a ship called the* Wellington, *dumped the dregs of their water barrels into Maui's warm streams. The mosquito had landed.*

Over the past one hundred and eighty years, avian malaria, along with habitat loss, has caused many bird extinctions in Hawaii. A few native birds survive at higher altitudes, where it's too cold for mosquitoes. But global warming has shoved the frost line higher up, reducing Hawaii's mosquito-free habitat.

INVADER – *Avian Malaria (alias Mosquito-Transmitted Avian Malarial Parasite)*

SIZE – *microscopic*

HOMELANDS – *Africa, Asia, South America*

LINE OF ATTACK – *avian malaria likely entered Hawaii via symptom-free domestic birds. When the mosquito arrived, avian malaria spread from domesticated bird, through mosquito, to wild bird, in a sick game of tag.*

AT HOME ON THE RANGE

Settlers found good pasture for their livestock on the North American prairies. Nutritious, native grasses grow in thick clumps, well-adapted to the wind and soil. But knapweed and leafy spurge put down deep taproots between clumps, guzzle up precious water, and leave native grasses to die of thirst. Cattle avoid eating leafy spurge because they seem to know it is toxic, but will eat knapweed, even though it, too, contains poisons and bears spines that injure their mouths. Today, ranchers find they can feed fewer cattle on the range where knapweed and leafy spurge have claimed squatter's rights.

INVADER – *Diffuse Knapweed (alias Tumbleweed)*

SIZE – *up to 1 m (3.3 ft.) tall*

HOMELANDS – *central and eastern Europe*

INVADER – *Leafy Spurge (alias Wolf's Milk)*

SIZE – *5 to 90 cm (2 to 35.4 in.) tall*

HOMELANDS – *Europe, central Asia*

LINE OF ATTACK – *early settlers of the western North American prairie carried knapweed and leafy spurge seeds from the Old World, mixed up in bags of grain they intended to sow on their new farms. Both plants spread quickly: In late summer leafy spurge pods explode, shooting seeds in all directions, while old knapweed plants tumble across open spaces in the wind, dropping seeds as they spin.*

Meanwhile, where stable and horn flies swarm unchecked, cattle spend more time whisking off the pests than they do eating. Even calves suffer because their mothers produce less milk. In Canada alone, billions of dollars are lost each year in beef, milk, and hay production because of these toxic plants and nasty flies.

INVADER – *Stable Fly (alias Dog Fly)*

SIZE – *8 mm (.3 in.) long*

HOMELAND – *North Africa*

INVADER – *Horn Fly (alias Cow Fly)*

SIZE – *5 mm (.2 in.) long*

HOMELAND – *Europe*

LINE OF ATTACK – *these biting flies sailed to North America in ships, feasting on the lifeblood of the horses and cows on which they piggybacked across the ocean.*

THE GREAT LAKES:
ONE INVASION AFTER ANOTHER

The Great Lakes hold one-fifth of the world's freshwater. For years, people blamed sewage, wastewater, and chemical dumping for killing the fish and polluting the lakes. Scientists now believe alien invaders are responsible too.

The sea lamprey – a jawless, boneless, scaleless fish – has a mouth shaped like an O, studded with rings of needle teeth. A slithery vampire, it attaches onto healthy fish and sucks out blood, then tissue, and finally bone. Sea lampreys killed millions of lake trout and walleye in the 1950s and drove three species of whitefish to extinc-

tion. When the larger fish disappeared, small invading fish called alewives suddenly had no predators and exploded in numbers. Alewives are prone to die off in great numbers and their stinking carcasses litter shorelines.

INVADER – *Sea Lamprey (alias Lamprey Eel)*

SIZE – *30 to 50 cm (11.8 to 19.7 in.) long*

HOME WATERS – *North Atlantic coastlines, western Mediterranean Sea*

LINE OF ATTACK – *sea lampreys may have shot the rapids near Montreal in the past and thrived in Lake Ontario for centuries, but Niagara Falls stopped them from swimming further inland. When the Erie and Welland canals opened in the 1820s, sea lampreys swam around the Falls into the upper four Great Lakes for the first time.*

41

A female zebra mussel can release over a million eggs a year – literally billions of adults now tile the Great Lake bottoms. Although they are small, such huge numbers of zebra mussels outcompete young fish for food, causing a decline in many species. Invading mussels attach onto native clams so thickly, the clams can't open their shells to feed – no wonder they are vanishing. Colonies of mussels encrust water-intake pipes so that towns and industries must spend millions of dollars a year to clean them out. Perhaps worst of all, as zebra mussels feed, they filter the lake water and concentrate many pollutants in their own bodies. Round gobies, small invasive fish, devour so many zebra mussels that the ducks and fish that eat them get poisoned. That means the people who eat the ducks or fish are eating pollutants too.

Since the 1820s, about 170 invaders have entered the Great Lakes and 45 more are poised to attack. Scientists are scrambling to protect this valuable reservoir of freshwater from the unintended consequences of canal-building and shipping.

INVADER – *Zebra Mussel (alias Moule Zebra)*

SIZE – *up to 3 cm (1.2 in.) long*

HOME WATERS – *Black, Caspian, and Azov seas of Eurasia*

LINE OF ATTACK – *in the mid-1980s, a transatlantic freighter pumped water into its ballast tanks from a Eurasian harbor to steady the ship on high seas. When the crew emptied the tanks into Lake St. Clair at the end of the voyage, zebra mussel stowaways flushed out with the water. Spread by currents and boats, those mussels colonized all the Great Lakes by 1990.*

THE EASTERN HARDWOOD FOREST

There's a pattering in the branches, telling you it's raining. But it's not water. Tiny fragments of leaves and insect poop are falling from the trees. Last year, flightless gypsy moths arrived in Southern Ontario via firewood and packing materials, on vehicles, or blew in on the wind. Each moth laid up to fifteen hundred eggs on the underside of tree limbs, in bark crevices, and on rocks. Most of the eggs survived the mild winter. Now millions of hungry caterpillars are stripping the leaves off the oak, maple, and hickory trees. And they'll find the hawthorn, willow, cherry, and apple trees at the meadow's edge.

Soon the sun will pound down on the forest floor, frying delicate plants that thrive in the shade. Many trees won't survive losing their leaves, especially those already stressed by global warming, wind or ice damage, and previous infestations.

Over time, invasive diseases have challenged many tree species in the North American eastern hardwood forests – eliminating elm, beech, and chestnut trees. Now the emerald ash borer is heading east, ignoring a ten-kilometer "ash-free" zone cut to contain them. The ash may soon be a species of the past, and with the gypsy moths at work, what's the future for the trees of the eastern hardwood forests?

INVADER – *European Gypsy Moth (alias Gypsy Moth)*

SIZE – *5.5 cm (2.2 in.) wingspan*

HOMELANDS – *Europe, North Africa*

INVADING – *eastern and central North America*

LINE OF ATTACK – *silk entrepreneur E. Léopold Trouvelot brought European gypsy moths to Massachusetts in 1868. A few escaped and, twenty years later, the first infestation was reported. Gypsy moths have been damaging eastern hardwood trees ever since.*

INVADER – *Emerald Ash Borer (alias EAB)*

SIZE – *8.5 to 14 mm (.3 to .5 in.) long*

HOMELAND – *eastern Asia*

INVADING – *United States, Canada*

LINE OF ATTACK – *eggs, larvae, or beetles of the emerald ash borer, hidden in wooden crates from Asia, turned up in Detroit, Michigan, in 2002 and soon flew east into Windsor, Canada, devastating millions of ash trees en route.*

Get Ready for the Pandemic

In early 1997, H5N1 avian flu struck chickens in rural Hong Kong. In May 1997, a three-year-old boy was diagnosed with the first human case of bird flu. He died, along with five others. A market selling live birds was blamed for the outbreak, and Hong Kong authorities killed the entire poultry population – 1.5 million domestic birds – stopping the virus dead in its tracks. But another strain of H5N1 popped up in Hong Kong poultry in 2001. Again, birds were slaughtered. This time the bird flu broke out almost immediately because the virus was still active in poultry living next door, in southern China.

Scientists observe a similarity between the H5N1 avian flu and the Spanish flu pandemic of 1918. Near the end of World War I, an American soldier got the flu. Troop ships took the virus to Europe and, within a year, half the world's population got sick and about 50 million died. Studies suggest that the Spanish flu started in birds and spread to humans, who had no immunities against this bird flu.

Flu viruses mutate (change) rapidly, allowing them to attack hosts that can't defend themselves. Flu vaccines are updated every year to cope with these changes. H5N1 is on the move across Asia and eastern Europe, but, as yet, does not readily transmit from one person to another. If or when it does, it will take months to develop a vaccine. And, with today's global travel and huge world population, H5N1 avian flu could become the worst pandemic in history.

INVADER – *H5N1 Avian Flu (alias Bird Flu)*

SIZE – *microscopic*

HOMELANDS – *east Asia and Southeast Asia*

INVADING – *Europe*

LINE OF ATTACK – *H5N1 avian flu virus is moving from Asia to Europe, with live poultry and wild birds. Why is the H5N1 virus threatening? Unlike most flu viruses, it jumps from one species to another – from birds to people.*

WHO CARES?

THEY'RE HERE, THEY'RE THERE, THEY'RE EVERYWHERE!

Alien invaders are a worldwide concern. In fact, many regions swap invaders back and forth. Here are a few examples:

Pinewood nematode

Gray squirrel

American comb jelly

Cannibal snail

Fire ant

Golden apple snail

 While zebra mussels from the Black, Caspian, and Azov seas infest the Great Lakes, American comb jellies from the eastern seaboard invade zebra mussels' home waters. These carnivorous jellyfish feast on fish eggs and young, threatening fisheries in all three seas.

 European sailing ships dispersed rats worldwide – now North American gray squirrels are the "forest rats" of England and Italy, driving red squirrels to local extinctions.

North America fears an attack on maple trees by Asian long-horned beetles as Japan fights pine wilt disease, carried by a North American worm called the pinewood nematode. Watching the devastation of Japanese forests, China braces for an assault.

 Snails are on the move. While giant African snails from East Africa invade tropical countries around the world, including Brazil, golden apple snails from Brazil menace the rice paddies of Southeast Asia and the United States. Cannibal snails from the southeastern United States, introduced in many countries to check giant African snails, are now killing off native snails, especially in the South Pacific.

Yellow crazy ants from Africa and Asia invade hot countries, including Brazil and the Caribbean island nations, just as fire ants from Central and South America march into North America, western Africa, and the Pacific Islands, killing insects, small animals, and even hatchling tortoises.

 European green crabs gobble up available food along temperate coastlines around the world, where the water temperature is moderate, while invading Chinese mitten crabs gorge in European waters.

 New Zealand and Australia have suffered multiple extinctions after invasions of dozens of animals and hundreds of plants, many from Europe. New Zealand now considers foreign species a matter of national security. Meanwhile, in Switzerland, the tiny New Zealand mud snail has morphed in Lake Zurich to over a half-million snails per square meter (10.8 sq. ft.). And an Australian barnacle threatens European coastlines.

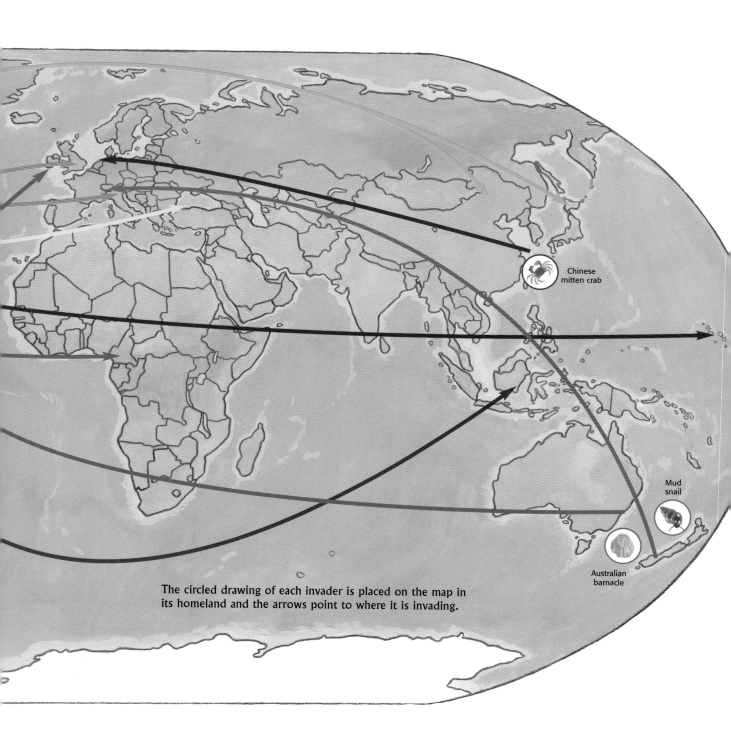

Chinese
mitten crab

Mud
snail

Australian
barnacle

The circled drawing of each invader is placed on the map in
its homeland and the arrows point to where it is invading.

49

WHAT'S THE BIG DEAL?

A healthy environment is home to plants and animals, including people. Each species needs its share of sunlight, water, food, air, and space. In return, the plants and animals give back – offering shade, storing water, becoming food, freshening the air, and creating hiding places. Native species develop special features, or adaptations, to better survive in the give-and-take of their living environment. The whole community becomes a life-support system for its members. Natural communities with many different species – that is, those rich in biodiversity – are the strongest and best able to bounce back from stress or disaster.

Invaders can weaken biodiversity, especially when they have no predators, diseases, parasites, or competitors in their new homes. They are usually aggressive and adaptable: They grow fast, reproduce in large numbers, handle long-distance travel, tolerate different temperatures, aren't fussy eaters, and don't mind people. Successful invaders take over available light, water, food, air, and space, pushing out native plants and animals, driving some to extinction. Although some habitats find ways to accommodate certain invaders, many don't and the natural community weakens.

People help invaders enfeeble biodiversity, usually by mistake. Road, canal, and city construction creates space ripe for stray seeds. Previous invasions caused by humans pave the way for sequels, particularly if predators are eliminated. And now scientists think global warming puts stress on species adapted to cooler temperatures, allowing invaders to barge in and take over.

In the long run, maybe over thousands of years, Nature will balance herself again. But, in the meantime, families of loggers and farmers and fishers suffer when alien invaders attack their home forests, fields, rivers, lakes, and seas. And it costs all of us when our governments spend huge amounts of tax dollars to control invasions.

Plants and animals thrive in a healthy home – and so do people.

51

WANTED: VOLUNTEERS

Scotch broom has spread across North America from Nova Scotia to Georgia in the east, and from California to Vancouver Island in the west. Sheep and goats are among the few creatures that eat its spiny leaves. Considered invasive in some areas and a weed in others, broom robs wildlife of food by choking out native plants.

On Vancouver Island, gangs of volunteers "broom bash" year-round. From fall to spring, they pull broom out by the roots. In summer, when dry conditions make the soil too hard to yank out the plants, broom bashers nip the buds, preventing seed dispersal.

INVADER – *Scotch Broom (alias Broom)*

SIZE – *1 to 2 m (3 to 6 ft.) tall*

HOMELANDS – *British Isles, central and southern Europe*

INVADING – *temperate, coastal North America*

LINE OF ATTACK – *sentimental settlers brought broom from their native Europe in the mid–1800s, planting it in gardens and to curb erosion.*

Soon after its arrival, kudzu became a popular hay substitute in the southern United States. Farmers were even paid by the Soil Conservation Service for planting this fast-growing vine. Today kudzu runs wild, suffocating many native plants in its path. Large swaths of Georgia, Mississippi, and Alabama grow nothing else. The vines twist up trees, smother their hosts, and flourish as ghostly kudzu "mummies."

High school students fight kudzu in South Carolina, earning community-service hours at the same time. "Kudzu parties" include cutting out the crowns of kudzu vines and testing new, nonchemical methods for exterminating the vines. When the job is done, the kids can swing, Tarzan-style, on the tougher vines.

INVADER – *Kudzu (alias Foot-a-Night Vine)*

SIZE – *leaves vary from 7 to 25 cm (2.7 to 9.8 in.) long; vines grow 18 m (59 ft.) per year*

HOMELANDS – *eastern Asia, Japan*

INVADING – *United States, South Africa, Malaysia, western Pacific islands*

LINE OF ATTACK – *kudzu plants were introduced to America at the Philadelphia Centennial Exposition in 1876.*

LESSONS LEARNED

Any team player will tell you that the best defense is a good offense. We have learned from every invasive outbreak – sometimes our solutions failed or made matters worse, but the game isn't over yet. Defeating alien invaders can start with you.

On nature's squad *(see pages 6, 14, 34)*
- Although Eugene Scheiffelin deliberately introduced starlings to North America, he didn't mean to start an invasion. Nature is usually more complex than you expect, so keep pets as pets and leave wild creatures alone.
- Question anyone introducing exotic plants or animals, even to get rid of pests. Natural, biological control can knock nature off balance.

Ecocoaching *(see pages 8–11)*
- Environmentally active elders in your neighborhood have lots of stories and wisdom to share. You're never too young, or too old, to be an ecoguardian.

Cut from the team *(see pages 12, 37)*
- Don't invite a rat for dinner by tossing unwanted food – even an apple core – on the ground.
- Help control the rat population by storing garbage securely, monitoring bird feeders, and composting properly.
- No matter where you live, discourage mosquitoes by emptying, cleaning, and refilling outdoor pet water dishes and birdbaths daily.

Home base *(see pages 16-17, 25)*
- If you travel, even within your own country, never take food, plants with seeds, or soil.
- Leave behind any interesting specimens – they belong where you found them. It took ten years and a million dollars to rid Florida of giant African snails when a child brought three back from his vacation.

Blow the whistle on invasive species *(see pages 18–19, 32–33, 44–45, 48–49)*
- Write your local government and demand strict regulations for nearby aquarium suppliers or fish farms.
- Report any signs of insects, such as Asian long-horned beetles, on your neighborhood trees to your city or town officials.
- If you see masses of egg cases, call the forestry service of your local government.

Keep pets onside *(see pages 20-23, 25, 26–27)*

- If you want a cat, adopt a homeless one. Keep your cat indoors at dawn and dusk to prevent the killing of birds, and don't allow her to have kittens.
- Think twice before getting an exotic pet, especially a snake. When it gets too big or breaks loose, it quickly slithers into trouble.
- Never release aquarium pets into the wild, nor flush water plants from fish or pet tanks down the toilet or sink.

Check for stowaways *(see pages 28–29, 40–43)*

- Inspect fishing and boating equipment to remove weeds, green crabs, and other "cling-ons" before entering new waters.
- When you travel between lakes, inspect trailer tires, boat motors, fishing lines, life jackets, and buckets for anything that might harbor invaders. And that includes drops of water!

Root out the problem
(see pages 30–31, 38, 52–53)

- If purple loosestrife, or other invading plants, takes hold near your home, dig the plant out by the roots before it flowers. Rot the seeds in a plastic bag, then compost them.
- Form a team with family, friends, or neighbors, wear heavy-duty gloves, and pull out invading plants.

Join forces *(see pages 34–35, 52–53, 56)*

- Support conservation groups such as WWF (World Wildlife Fund) or Ducks Unlimited, which invest in local programs to control invasive species.
- Look up your federal, state/provincial, or local government. Browse their websites for invasive-species concerns in your community and volunteer your help.

Clean up your act *(see pages 46–47)*

- Wash your hands properly, and prevent the spread of illness. It takes about twenty seconds – the time needed to sing the alphabet – to get the job done.
- Sneeze in your sleeve when soap and water is not available.

INDEX

For more information on alien
invaders, use the Internet. A good
international site to check out
"100 of the worst" invaders is
http://www.issg.org/database.

To find out about alien invaders
attacking your community and
how you can help, type "invasive
species" in the search box on the
government website of your
country, province, state, county,
municipality, and/or town.